PLAYING POSSUM

Riddles about Kangaroos, Koalas, and Other Marsupials

by John Jansen
pictures by Susan Slattery Burke

Lerner Publications Company • Minneapolis

For Mick and Lauren —J.J.
To Nick, for all his love and support —S.S.B.

This book is available in two editions:
Library binding by Lerner Publications Company
Soft cover by First Avenue Editions
241 First Avenue North
Minneapolis, MN 55401

Library of Congress Cataloging-in-Publication Data

Jansen, John, 1956-
   Playing possum : riddles about kangaroos, koalas, and other
marsupials/by John Jansen ; pictures by Susan Slattery Burke.
      p.   cm. — (You must be joking!)
   ISBN 0-8225-2346-9 (lib. bdg.) ISBN 0-8225-9674-1 (pbk.)
   1. Riddles, Juvenile. 2. Marsupialia—Juvenile humor.
[1. Marsupials—Wit and humor. 2. Riddles. 3. Jokes.] I. Burke,
Susan Slattery, ill. II. Title. III. Series.
PN6371.5.J36 1995
398.6—dc20   94-19553

Manufactured in the United States of America

1 2 3 4 5 6 – I/JR – 00 99 98 97 96 95

Q: What do possums eat as they hang from trees?

A: Upside-down cake.

Q: What is the meanest marsupial?

A: The Tasmanian devil.

Q: What makes more noise than a Tasmanian devil?

A: Two Tasmanian devils.

Q: What mammal is born extremely immature, stays in its mother's pouch for months, eats fruit and flowers, and is real cool?

A: A possum on vacation at the North Pole.

Q: What's the difference between the North American opossum and the Australian possum?

A: The letter "o."

Q: What marsupial eats grass and stings?

A: A walla-bee.

Q: What do you get when you cross a wallaby with a clock?

A: A pocket watch.

Q: What do you call a bat
   that wears a big
   wool sweater?

A: A wombat.

Q: Why are wombats
   always in debt?

A: Because they are
   burrowers.

Q: What sport does a
   wallaby play?

A: Wally-ball.

Q: How did the kangaroo exercise?

A: She did her jumping jacks.

Q: Why are kangaroos such good workers?

A: They always hop to it.

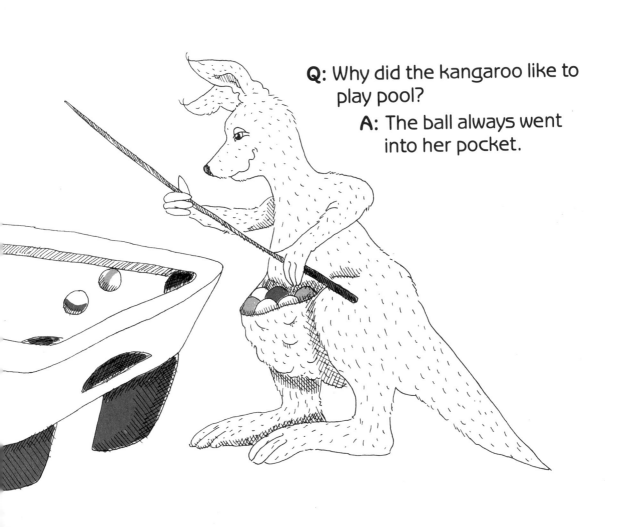

Q: Why did the kangaroo like to play pool?

A: The ball always went into her pocket.

Q: Was the kangaroo nervous?
A: No, she was just a little jumpy.

Q: What do marsupials have that no other animal can have?
A: Baby marsupials.

Q: What marsupial grows the fastest?
A: The kangaroo. It grows by leaps and bounds.

Q: Can you name eight marsupials?
A: A wombat, an opossum, a koala, a wallaby, a bandicoot, and three kangaroos.

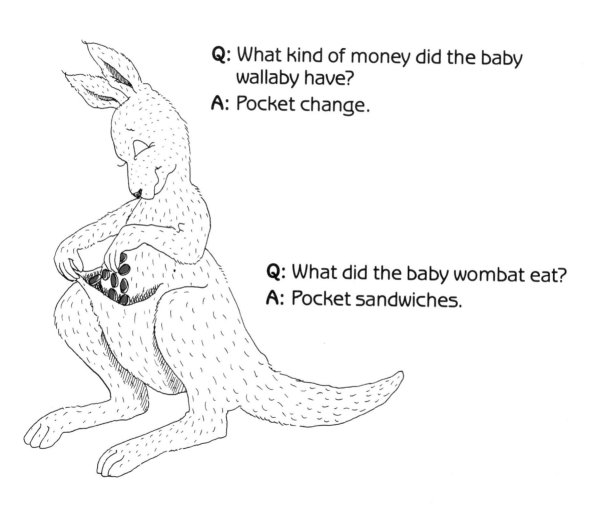

Q: What kind of money did the baby wallaby have?

A: Pocket change.

Q: What did the baby wombat eat?

A: Pocket sandwiches.

Q: How do you stop a kangaroo from jumping on your bed at noon?

A: Take him outside at eleven.

Q: What time is it when a kangaroo jumps on your sofa?

A: Time to buy a new sofa.

Q: What looks like a large rat, like a bandicoot, with a long pointed nose, like a bandicoot, but is *not* a bandicoot?

A: A picture of a bandicoot.

Q: What's the difference between a cheerleader and a bandicoot?

A: One roots for the team, the other roots for insects.

Q: What do you say to a baby marsupial?

A: Bandi-cootchy-cootchy-coo.

Q: Why was the bandicoot's uncle so upset?

A: Because the bandicoot eats ants.

Q: What happens if a bandicoot eats too many ants?
A: He has to take an ant-acid.

Q: Why was the mama kangaroo angry with the baby kangaroo?

A: He was eating crackers in bed.

Q: Why was the baby wombat called "Cue Ball"?
A: He was small, bald, and ended up in the pocket.

Q: Why shouldn't you give a baby marsupial a hairbrush?
A: Because he'll never part with it.

Q: How did the baby bandicoot keep his bed neat?
A: With a pocket comb.

Q: Why did the baby wombat feel bad?
A: His mother was always looking down on him.

Q: Why did the baby wombat giggle and laugh?
A: She was tickled by the pouch fuzz.

Q: What is the marsupial's favorite dance?

A: The tango-roo.

Q: What is the kangaroo's favorite kind of dance music?

A: Hip-hop.

Q: What is the kangaroo's favorite game?

A: Checkers. He likes to jump.

Q: What would you get if you crossed an elephant with a kangaroo?

A: A lot of big holes all over Australia.

Q: What did the koala call the boomerang that didn't come back?

A: A stick.

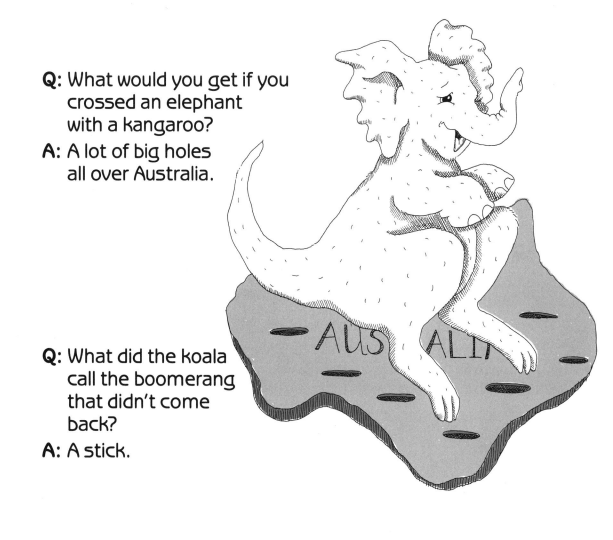

Q: What happened when the wallaby got a new boomerang?

A: He went crazy trying to throw the old one away.

Q: What kind of pants do wallabies wear?

A: Crocodile dungarees.

Q: Which has more legs: a kangaroo or no kangaroo?

A: No kangaroo. A kangaroo has four legs, but no kangaroo has six legs.

Q: Why do Feathertail possums live only on the island of New Guinea?

A: They don't like to swim.

Q: Why did the koala's dinner walk away?

A: Because eucalyptus leaves.

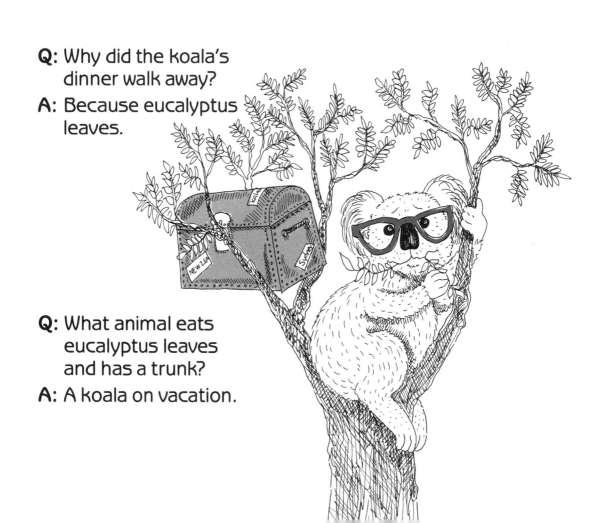

Q: What animal eats eucalyptus leaves and has a trunk?

A: A koala on vacation.

Q: How do you catch a koala?
A: Hide behind a tree and make noises like eucalyptus leaves.

Q: Is eating eucalyptus good for your eyes?
A: Sure. Did you ever see a koala with glasses?

Q: What is the koala's favorite planet?
A: Mars-upial.

Q: Who is the leader of the marsupials?
A: The kangaroo-ler.

Q: Why didn't the kangaroo move?
A: He knew no bounds.

Q: What kind of raincoat does the wallaby wear?

A: A poucho.

Q: Why do mother bandicoots hate rainy days?

A: Because the children have to play inside.

Q: What goes "hop-squish, hop-squish, hop-squish?"
A: A kangaroo wearing a wet sneaker.

Q: What's hot and steamy and filled with bandicoots?
A: Mar-soup-ials.

Q: What's a bad appetizer at a marsupial party?
A: Tazmanian deviled eggs.

Q: How can you tell if there's a kangaroo in the refrigerator?
A: The refrigerator door won't close.

Q: Why was the possum arrested?
A: Because she was a pickpocket.

Q: What sound did the marsupial's bell make?
A: Clangaroo.

Q: What do you call a marsupial marching band?
A: The Bandicoots.

Q: What do you call a bandicoot who watches TV all day long?
A: A pouch potato.

Q: What's the kangaroo's favorite year?
A: Leap year.

Q: What is the kangaroo's favorite kind of bread?
A: Hoppyseed.

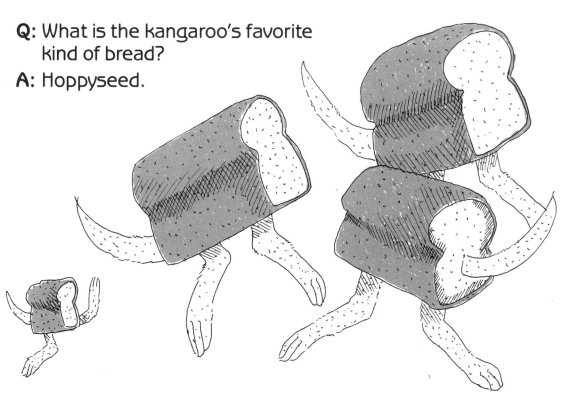

Q: Why did the kangaroo sit on a Mother Goose book?
A: Because kangaroos always sit on their tales.

Q: Why do kangaroos sit on their tails?
A: They can't afford any furniture.

Q: What kind of a kangaroo can jump higher than a house?
A: Any kind. A house can't jump.

Q: What goes hop-bump-ouch, hop-bump-ouch?
A: A six-foot kangaroo in a seven-foot room.

Q: What is the koala's favorite musical instrument?
A: The ukelele-lyptus.

Q: What do marsupials sing at Christmas?
A: Koala-la-la-la, la-la-la-la.

Q: What do you call a kangaroo
that wears tie-dye?

A: A hoppy hippie.

Q: What happened to the
kangaroo prince and
princess?

A: They lived hoppily ever after.

ABOUT THE AUTHOR

John Jansen and his wife, Michele, live in Minneapolis, Minnesota. John writes video scripts and screenplays and has written and performed stand-up comedy. He loves to tell bedtime stories that make his kids, Mick and Lauren, laugh. He really hopes that you get a laugh or two out of this book.

ABOUT THE ARTIST

Susan Slattery Burke loves to illustrate fun-loving characters, especially animals. To her, each of her characters has a personality all its own. She is most satisfied when the characters come to life for the reader as well. Susan lives in Minnetonka, Minnesota, with her husband, two daughters, and their dog and cat. Susan enjoys sculpting, reading, traveling, illustrating, and chasing her children around.

You Must Be Joking books

Alphabatty
Riddles from A to Z

Class Act
Riddles for School

Help Wanted
Riddles about Jobs

Here's to Ewe
Riddles about Sheep

Hide and Shriek
Riddles about Ghosts
and Goblins

Ho Ho Ho!
Riddles about
Santa Claus

Home on the Range
Ranch-Style Riddles

Hoop-La
Riddles about Basketball

I Toad You So
Riddles about Frogs and Toads

Off Base
Riddles about Baseball

On with the Show
Show Me Riddles

Out on a Limb
Riddles about Trees
and Plants

Out to Dry
Riddles about Deserts

Playing Possum
Riddles about Kangaroos,
Koalas, and Other Marsupials

Plugged In
Electric Riddles

Summit Up
Riddles about Mountains

Take a Hike
Riddles about Football

That's for Shore
Riddles from the Beach

Weather or Not
Riddles for Rain and Shine

What's Gnu?
Riddles from the Zoo

Wing It!
Riddles about Birds